Witch Tree

A Collaboration

Witch Tree

A Collaboration

Words by Joanne Hart
Images by Hazel Belvo

HOLY COW! PRESS
DULUTH, MINNESOTA

FIRST PRINTING
10 9 8 7 6 5 4 3 2 1

Library of Congress Cataloging-in-Publication Data
Hart, Joanne.
    Witch tree: a collaboration / text by Joanne Hart; images by Hazel Belvo
        p.   cm.
    ISBN 0-930100-46-8 (Paperback)
    1. Indians of North America—Minnesota—Poetry. 2. Grand Portage
(Minn.)—Poetry 3. Trees—Poetry. I. Belvo, Hazel, 1934- .
    II. Title.
    PS3558.A6817W5   1992
    811' .54—dc20   91—73629
                                             CIP

Publisher's Address: Distributor's Address:
Holy Cow! Press   The Talman Company, Inc.
Post Office Box 3170   150 Fifth Avenue
Mount Royal Station   New York, New York 10011
Duluth, Minnesota 55803

This project is supported, in part, by a grant from the National Endowment for the Arts in Washington, D.C.,
a Federal agency.

ACKNOWLEDGEMENTS

Versions of some of these poems have appeared in the following journals:
> *Sing Heavenly Muse!, Great River Review, Dacotah Territory, Milkweed Chronicle, WARM Journal, Verbal Events, Loonfeather, The South Dakota Review, Touchstone.*

"Fog," "Survival" and "Signs" were originally published in *The Village Schoolmaster* (The Bieler Press, 1985). I appreciate the permission of Gerald Lange to include them here. "Gatherers" and "Scenic Look-out" were first published by Women's Times Publishing as broadsides and are available from the artist, Betsy Bowen, Grand Marais, Minnesota 55604. "Elders," written for Catherine Lupori, was reprinted in *Anthology of Magazine Verse & Yearbook of American Poetry 1981.*

I am grateful to Barton Sutter for permission to quote from his poem "Witch Tree" (*Pine Creek Parish Hall*, Sandhills Press: Ord, Nebraska, 1985); to the Minnesota Historical Society for access to "A Grand Portage Story and Other Tales from the North Country" (1963), a typescript of Dewey Albinson's memoirs; to Patricia Harpole, librarian at the Minnesota Historical Society, and to Karen Evens, librarian at the Grand Portage National Monument, for help with my research.

Many people helped to open my eyes to the traditions surrounding the Witch Tree. I wish to express my gratitude in particular to Hazel Belvo, to George Morrison and to Rick Novitsky. I am grateful to Nancy and Roger Lienke, Billy Blackwell and Herman and Penny Hendrickson for their patience with my questions and their loan of materals. Cynthia Driscoll provided me with the statement of wood artist, Mary Thouin. Ron Drude, with his story of drought, and John Reinhard, with his poet's challenge, gave me the impetus to write my first poem about the tree.

I am grateful to Jill Breckenridge, Gillian Conoley, Elizabeth Erickson, Mary Jean Port, Francine Sterle, Barton Sutter and Mark Vinz for their generous response when I asked for criticism, and to Nathaniel Hart, who gave me, as always, encouragement, criticism and loving support.

Joanne Hart

Barbara Gilhooly printed these relief blocks at the Minneapolis College of Art and Design print shop. Judy Stone Nunneley and Elizabeth Erickson gave me excellent criticism and encouragement in my experience with this new medium.

I am grateful to Marcia Casey Cushmore, who addressed with me my philosophical concerns about the "Meditation on the Spirit Tree" and gives me constant support.

I am thankful to my friends, Mary Morrison Dahmen, Ellen Olson, Jaune Quick-to-See Smith, Arlene Dearing, Penny Hendrickson, Nancy Lienke and Mike Morrison, who have given me the insight into Native American beliefs necessary to my creative work.

I am grateful to the artist, George Morrison, for the gift of his culture to me. Our son, Briand Mesaba, embodies our two cultures: my Dutch-American farm and his father's Native American Chippewa. It was George who first brought me to the tree.

Hazel Belvo

We dedicate this book to the people of Grand Portage

ORDER OF CONTENTS

GLOSSARY

ah-say-ma ▲ tobacco

Anishinabe (*Anishinabeg*, plural) ▲ The People, the tribal name of the Indians commonly called Chippewa, Ojibwa or Ojibway

Ma-ni-do ▲ Spirit, or more accurately Mystery. Basil Johnston writes, "The term could be applied to natural settings which had some special atmosphere about them . . ." (*Ojibway Ceremonies*, University of Nebraska Press, 1990; pg. 30)

Ma-ni-do Gee-zhi-gance ▲ Spirit (or Mystery) Little Cedar Tree, the traditional name for the Grand Portage Witch Tree

Minong ▲ Good Place, the traditional name for Isle Royale

No-ko-mis ▲ Grandmother

Waus-wau-goning ▲ Place of torch fishing, the name of the bay overlooked by the Witch Tree, northeast of Grand Portage and Hat Point

AUTHOR'S STATEMENT

Returned from a short walk to the Witch Tree, we sit perched on high stools in Hazel Belvo's Grand
Portage studio which looks out over Lake Superior. Hazel has her notebook open and I have my
yellow pad before me on the drafting table. The one hour we had expected to spend together has
extended to five as Hazel shows me paintings and portfolios of drawings. I read aloud my poems.
We talk, reaching deep into the inner consciousness, telling what the spirit of the tree means to
each of us, describing our creative experiences and our work.

This 1989 session of mutual exploration was the first of only half a dozen times we talked, because Hazel's
job keeps her in Minneapolis and I write at home in Grand Portage. But the mysterious process
of creative collaboration, fed by these infrequent meetings, continued for two years across 300
miles. Occasionally I sent a batch of poems to Hazel, once in a while we wrote to each other, but
the agreement was that neither of us would be the "illustrator" of the other's work—each would
bring creative response to the subject we discussed together, the Spirit Tree. Hazel opened my
imagination to ideas and physical presences—rock shapes, sky colors, textures of bark—I did not
see before we began our story-making. As we continued our work on the book, she gave me an
early engraving of the rock passage to the tree. I gave her more and more poems.

When we first spoke of collaboration, I had been working for about a year with Friends of the Witch Tree,
telling the story of Spirit Little Cedar, *Ma-ni-do Gee-zhi-gance*, to people who might be moved to
donate to a fund drive and save the Witch Tree site from the commercial real estate market. Hazel,
too, was active in the fund drive effort to save the tree, but she had experienced many years of
artistic and spiritual connection with the Witch Tree, the subject of a significant body of her work.
It was Hazel who first alerted me to the traditional spirit place on Hat Point when I interviewed
her and painter, George Morrison, for a *Lake Superior Magazine* feature in 1986. Without that
introduction, I would not have known the importance of the tree for the Grand Portage Chippewa
Band and for the international arts community.

Learning that there was no significant published resource on the Witch Tree other than two articles in
Minnesota Volunteer, the magazine of the state Department of Natural Resources, I turned to
several friends in Grand Portage who could give me the information I needed. Herman and Penny
Hendrickson, Grand Portage Band members who inherited the land where the Witch Tree grows,
told me many details of their life on the reservation. Nancy Lienke, an anthropologist who did

research interviews at Grand Portage in the 1960's, now lives on the Grand Portage Bay Road with her husband, Dr. Roger Lienke. She loaned me materials, discussed the Spirit Cedar with me, and gave me the story of their friendship with the artist Dewey Albinson. I read the unpublished Albinson memoir, deposited in the Minnesota Historical Society, as well as letters and memorabilia from Nancy's files, and learned how Albinson gave the tree its common name, the Witch Tree, in the title of one of his paintings. Billy Blackwell, my Anishinabe neighbor, gave me valuable insights into the spiritual significance of the tree and loaned me materials about the custom of summer food-gathering on Isle Royale.

Gradually the story of the tree, its mythic significance, its history, and my own parallel story began to shape the book's sections. I was able to write of my life here and the changes that have come to me and my family as we made our home among the Grand Portage Anishinabeg. Despite the differences among us, we humans seek a common bond in the hope of understanding, but often we connect and recognize each other without words for what we share. It has been important for me to acknowledge what I have learned from living on the Reservation. I am taught over and over again to recognize and respect life—in the people, the changing boreal woods, in wild animals and birds, the never-certain weather, the Northern Lights, in the Pigeon River cutting through Precambrian rock by my cabin and dropping toward the great lake.

As I learned about the tree, I realized people are awed that it continues to live, for hundreds of years, despite seemingly impossible conditions. I am indebted to Basil Johnston's fine book, *Ojibway Heritage* (University of Nebraska Press, 1990), for reminding me that rock, wind, water and fire are the basic substances of life bestowed by the initial creative act of the Great Spirit. They are mysteriously manifest in the tree and its setting. It seems appropriate, then, to divide this book into four sections—Rock, Wind, Water, Fire—in order to describe tribal culture still strong on the Reservation, as well as my personal experiences and my learned understanding of life in Grand Portage. The Witch Tree is both symbol and living reality of the Place, the Spirit here, the People whom I know, and the creative fire of Art that springs from this strange and beautiful cedar.

ARTIST'S STATEMENT

When I was a child, on our Southern Ohio farm we had a pond surrounded by dense trees and
undergrowth. The gnarled roots of the trees turned and twisted into the water. I arranged my
treasures—stones, beads, bits of cloth and sticks, clothes pins and precious objects—in small tin
boxes and carefully hid them under the roots of the trees. Regularly I visited them in their secret
places, rearranging, adding, and changing. At night, terrified of the dark, I lay in my bed thinking
of my boxes in their safe hiding places at the roots of the trees, and somehow I felt connected to
the universe, at peace in the night. Jung recalls a similar experience in his book, *Dreams,
Memories, and Reflections.* At times of extreme anxiety, like Jung remembering his treasured
carving, visualizing it in its hiding place, I felt reassured of my own place in the universe.

In 1961, when I first came to the Grand Portage Spirit Tree and laid the traditional gift of tobacco at its
base, I felt a return to my spiritual home. I again connected to a higher power in our universe that
is far older than I am. The tree, *No-ko-mis,* and the people of Grand Portage have taught me
through thirty years that a gift to the tree asks for power, a power neither good nor bad, but defined
by the person who uses it. How right this is for my belief system. I realize that beginning from my
childhood farm home and values, moving through the educational system, the New York art
world and the modern industrial, technological world, my travels have brought me here to this
tree. A young spiritual leader of the Chippewa people once said to me, "When your magic appears
to you, you will recognize it." The tree is that magic, the key to my artistic metaphor. More than
the Spirit Tree itself, the metaphor is the journey of life. My creative work has stemmed from this
metaphor for the past twelve years.

As I have drawn, photographed and painted the tree, the meaning of the metaphor has come to me.
"Meditation on the Spirit Tree" is a large body of work that I began in 1979. The work has seven
parts: The Path, The Passage, The Rock, The Root, The Torso, The Crown, The Tree/Spirit.

The Path ▲ From the road I walk through a meadow dotted with flowers, insects, pebbles, ice in winter and open space, then through a rain forest, a tunnel of tall trees, lush undergrowth, textures and colors of moss, mushrooms, flowers and animal homes. Overhead the bearded lichen hangs, and many trees are diagonal in their return to earth. The process from birth through life to death and transformation is visually manifest in the path. At first I was saddened by the decay, but over time I rejoiced in the life it gives the forest.

The Passage ▲ At the end of the path stand two large, body-sized rocks through which I must pass to climb down where the tree grows. The rocks are dark against the brightness of the sky and water, so that I pass into the light, whether day or night. Once through the passage, I look back and see the rocks, light against the darkness of the forest. This is rebirth and remembrance. Without the dark, what is light?

The Rock ▲ The tree grows out of a rock bed at the edge of formidable Lake Superior. The rock, covered with orange lichen, hangs, a cliff over the water. Here the water moves in circlets, whirlpools, dangerous, compelling. This place is for understanding, a place for reflecting. In the water is the reflection of the tree.

The Root ▲ Over the rock flows a petrified piece of the tree, a root, awesome, transcending life and death. A mystery: is it alive or is it dead? Rippling, silvery, soft, hard, tough, this old root of the past exists simultaneously with the tree's deeper, nourishing roots embedded somewhere in Mother Earth.

The Torso ▲ The body or stem of the Spirit Tree twists, voluptuous, old. Curving up and out, this is a body to embrace, a body to respect, a body whose visual manifestation is her own deep memory, her experiences. She knows generations of wisdom. What has happened here? I see a body gestating, for the essential process of life is gestation.

The Crown ▲ The top of the tree remains ever green even at fifty degrees below zero. Darkening, showing rusty brown, yet always becoming bright with new growth spread toward the sun, the branches are antennae to the universe. Here is the exchange I marveled at when, as a child, I learned that plants breathe out what we animals breathe in, and we breathe out what plants breathe in. I marveled over this miracle—I still do.

The Tree/Spirit ▲ This wise One is our connection to the universe, the secret of survival. Here we remember life in harmony with all being, past, present, future. The reverence we feel is the full embodiment and practice of love. Until we have a global culture which understands and believes this, our entire planet and all its life is endangered.

Rock

SPIRIT LITTLE CEDAR TREE

THE PLACE

Catkins flower on birch and willow. Maple sugar season ends, and the Anishinabe families get ready to spend the summer at *Minong*, island of plenty. There the fat trout and sturgeon wait to swim into the fishing nets. Next month strawberries will grow plump in the long days of sunshine. Then Juneberries, blueberries, cranberries take their turns to sweeten. Beaver and caribou meat will hang on the drying racks.

The children are excited about the long trip on the lake. They will ride in the middle of the canoes with the dogs. Women pack maple sugar, wild rice, kettles for cooking, rolls of bark for wigwams to set up on the island. The men add nets, ammunition, guns. Before the sun rises, when the pre-dawn light shows them the smooth water under its trailing sleeve of mist, the loaded canoes begin the non-stop run from Waus-wau-goning Bay to the archipelago of *Minong*, the Good Place floating on Lake Superior twenty-two miles off shore.

▲ ▲ ▲

A seasonal journey was made year after year by canoe to Isle Royale, *Minong*, where Anishinabe families spent the summer months harvesting the wide variety of fish and game. Usually they returned to the mainland for wild rice season and stayed there for the winter. Members of only one extended family might use *Minong* as winter hunting ground and make the treacherous return trip to the island in autumn after the wild rice harvest. *Minong* was a rich, accessible resource to people who knew how to travel Lake Superior in birch bark canoes.

The Anishinabeg set out from Hat Point. There Spirit Little Cedar Tree, *Ma-ni-do Gee-zhi-gance*, still rises alone from a diabase rock platform at the lake shore. Huge boulders form a backdrop for the tree as it leans forward, raised a little, projected by its throne over the water. There seems to be no soil to nourish the heavy roots which enter cracks in the rock and grip. Foresters think the cedar could be 400 years old, a mysterious survival in such an exposed location where the tree is separated by a wide rock shelf from nutrients of the forest floor. This *ma-ni-do* may have received spirit offerings of the first Anishinabeg to settle in the northern Lake Superior area during the 17th century.

▲ ▲ ▲

The place we live, the old border crossing, was once a town on the Pigeon River with Customs house, cafe, tourist cabins. The land remains littered with human detritis: in the woods, dumps of tins and old medicine bottles; below the meadow, like an outcrop of bona fide rock, a ridge of oil cans and auto parts from the gas station. We gathered up car bodies and piles of broken appliances, hauled them away or buried them in the hole where a house once stood. Some heaps, overgrown with small trees and vines, seemed better left undisturbed. Even after years of picking up and disposing, each spring when the green undergrowth has not yet pushed through winter-flattened mulch, trash reveals itself. By the path where we have walked many seasons, suddenly a disintegrating boot and the brown shards of a broken beer bottle appear.

How hard for humans to fit into place, I think, as I pick up the pieces of glass. Discarded clothing, tools, utensils and sheltering structures once could decay back into the natural world they came from, but what we call modern technology has provided us with materials foreign to the places we drop them: the plastic diaper, the asphalt roofing, the steel spoon, the rubber tire all strangers to the north woods.

At first I felt possessive, owner of these acres of trees and river cliffs, owner of our home. But gradually as I listened to my Anishinabe friends, it came to me that "home" is a figment in the traveler's mind, a place where one's language fits and references make sense. I can own this place only in my imagination, and everyone in Grand Portage owns it as well. Each of us stays on the land a little while; others will follow in their turn, here like trees and animals and then gone.

SCENIC LOOK-OUT

It's good that we can lie on rocks
and overlook the far Canadian hills.
See where the gap like a saddle
rides the Arrow waterfall
to the Pigeon River? Trees
and the rock shield they clothe
carve contours that seem
close, within our reach.
Like music—change of key,
harmonic phrases turned—
untouchable, the scene
for a moment
holds us in the mode of touching.

We are not the first ones made
that we should strive to name
the slug on its silver trail,
fox in the thicket, ridge,
pine, shining raven, sky,
the world laid out eons before
in ice and lava flow. Nor are we the ones
who will survive to catalog what's left.
Yet, together for this little while,
attuned to touch, we can look out
from height and recognize
the Garden on the old volcanic world.

PATH

Under layers of leaves and pine needles
earth lies thin, the subtle decay of years.
Ferns begin to brown in the waning light.
The sun slants lower toward a winter sky.
Birds signal change even before nights

start to lengthen. Warblers and their young
disguised in streaks and chevroned wings turn
from the brief frenzy of nesting and answer
the urge south. They leave a silent woods.
Light complicates the patterning of roots,

trees felled all one way by a freak wind.
The sun picks out scattered gold leaves,
a patch of red bearberry, green gloss near
a rock outcrop scaled with lichen grey.
Colors come forth into freckled light,

fade back. Nothing is still to the eye. The path
drops abruptly down the north slope.
Air chills. Beyond granite buttresses,
the portal widens to lichen, rock, cold sea.
Isle Royale, like a mirage floating

twenty miles off-shore, lifts from mist
and casts its cliffs and flaming maple hills
across the water toward Hat Point, the place
land and lake paths join. Here Spirit Cedar,
holding down a dark volcanic world,

signals across wide sky toward islands,
disappearing promises in mist,
toward changing light from scarlet sunrises,
moons drawing a white finger through water,
lightning flash, the Borealis dance.

A boat, set forth with courage, will return
on the water path—on stars, on spirit wells,
on glassy shallows and the sudden drop-off.
The deep, hidden power draws the map,
a shivering path over ribs and spine.

PATH TO THE SPIRIT TREE

F O G

From river rock cliffs,
lichen paint and fern,
many-colored walls of rock,
from foaming water over rapids
and the breathing waters
in the lake beyond the bay,
comes evening fog in columns
piled and joined, grown, rising,
rising to the lay of land.

Looking for a moment to the mountains,
to a touch of light,
to wooded curve and cleft of hills
and turning back, we feel
the grey advance.

Pines begin their beading
needlework of water drops
on this great shroud, cool
isolator,
river mantle,
fog.

TOWER ROCK

Wind cries across the cables
under the rockbound radio tower,
wind in wires following me.
I follow bears
over the brush-grown mother rock
where bushes fruit Juneberries
big as grapes, and sweet.
Here and there a bush is mangled,
bear-crushed, broken.
—Pull the bush down. Strip
with clawed hands. Stuff leaves, fruit
onto a blue tongue.

Travel berry long ago, to carry
courting across miles of woods,
food for the hunt, Juneberries,
drop now into my bucket
toward winter and dark afternoons,
drop into my blue mouth
the pale taste of rock and steel.

How the wind cries in girders, across the cables.

I think of women brought to rutted frontier streets,
through raw mud, Dakota spring break up,
women tied to farm wagons, wind-battered
wild as prairies they sought to tame.
—At the reins, a man rigid with watchfulness,
children beside him shadowed

winter-grey around the eyes,
behind, a she-bear chained but feared,
his woman mad with wind, snow, sky.

Here in pines wind sounds before
I notice bushes toss or feel
a chill against my face.
The northern forest sings the wind,
but up this tower rock I hear
blowing from the prairie west
a thin, high, scream.

LETTERS

Saving your letters keeps a hold
at the pole of this whirling world. No
bold language between us, nothing unfit
for the children's eyes, your catalog of days.
Love shows its subtle patterned code
over years, the way a woods we know
has slowly changed, trees tall as you
grown in our road, the stream diverted,
marshes drained. Birds return each spring,
but in renewal, not all the same.

A warbler, window-dashed, a rag now,
hangs in my hand flattened, flagged. I think
of bird-lovers who meet in spring migration,
dusk and dawn, on a prairie rise where a tower
plants cables and girders like a net.
Fields all around lie plowed, drilled, seeded.
The lovers come for body counts,
dead species for life lists.
Up the steel shaft red lights flash-warn-flash
into the wide sky to the whispering ones,
endangered flocks, travelers high above
bent backs of birders counting males
who would not inseminate females
who would not lay that year,
listing the loss.

Do you believe in me—or I in you?
The question is old as spring and pied

as breeding plumage with a thousand
ways to answer. Someone of our kind
in a distant dusk will spell it out,
like checking old records of birds,
the seasons of your letters I saved.

BIRDS

Canada geese shouting, beating
south under a low sky.
The harsh bright bell of jays.
Remembered cries
I learned lying in a meadow,
swooning into clouds.
My heart lifts, body freezes
at the scream of a red-tailed
hawk quartering the sky.
Is the heart's leap a push to flight?
Some mad ones strap on
wax and feathers, metal wings, and try.

I used to color birds in books
crayola red and blue. When I saw
study skins in drawers
and I could take up in my hand
markings, the lesson of feathers,
I corrected for beauty,
but the birds were as remote as if
they flew under the cloud
and I were watching.

The shock of recognition comes late for me
who thought I learned the birds:
I face a jessed hawk panting on the wrist.
Its breath is hot as mine. And near
the red pine suet cage I hear
the cut of wing through wind,
the loud, hard, unexpected sound
of beating on this substance, air.

LUCK

Beyond the spring where the road rises,
a black fox leaps across, sails in an arc
before me like a catapulted stone—
eyes and mask like coal, no frosted hairs
over the long sinews of its shadow
body but the tell-tale white tip flare
at the end of the arc. Henry, who lives
with changeling weasles and a she-bear greyed
by years of cubs, says black fox
he's heard of, never seen—luck, my luck.

By the road to Partridge Falls, three times,
a woodpecker, broad white across the wings,
immature, a puzzle here, flicks
to the dead top of a pine. The risen river
threatens at my step, drowns familiar rocks,
sweeps the grassy island of wild mint,
tongues through hazy autumn night like lovers
in their sleeplessness, murmuring,
waiting for the moon to set, dreading
winter dawns ahead, cold months apart.

I am afraid of what I want to see.
As prairie dusk drops into dark, I walk
the street where we used to live together.
I choose not to recognize the house:
trees are gone, hedges grown, yellow siding
masks the face. But in the dimming gleam
of evening, rain clouds boiling along
the vast horizon and a street lamp showing
more intense in shadows, I pick up
the sharp musk smell, how we lived, the luck.

PASSAGE TO THE SPIRIT TREE

SERPENT

Mary and I mount the side
of Josephine, climb steeply past
boletas on the path, stop
to breathe the moist, dark flank,
the mothersmell of earth and green.
Through maple, thimbleberry, pine,
this trail could be the track of moose,
strong-haunched climbers, sure-footed
on rock and duff, heads high, at ease,
graceful in their bulky weight.

We clamber, bracing at the drop,
panting, knocking against our thighs
the empty buckets we bring to pick
blueberries. Mount Josephine,
serpent of lava and old bones,
stretches toward the watery cleft
she came from—belched forth hissing,
flung to lie stunned on the shore—
a basalt dike with serpent's spine,
her threatening head bent to the lake.

The top of the ridge is lizard scale:
furze and lichened rock. Hot sun.
Under our hands we feel old fire.
Islands lie like fishing boats,
clouds flicked out like nets flung wide,
all around us plenitude.
Blue sky, blue lake, blue fruited field.
We won't forget a day when we
could pick our fill of blueberries
and dare to ride a serpent's back.

MA-NI-DO GEE-ZHI-GANCE

Prairie noon turns black. The woman lights her lamps.
What cycle, she wonders, what perversity lets wind
dry the earth and take it, shroud the light from air?

Knowing how stone works through seasons to topsoil
and plow, calling in a backhoe, digging to give
a pile of stumps final rest, in ten feet,

fifteen, the farmer finds no sign of dampness. Bone
dry. A handful of his field shapes smooth as talc,
powdered fine to fill the hand of wind. Silt

drifts across the road like black windrows of snow.
He's afraid to till or seed the ghostly fields.
If nothing can decay, he says, nothing can grow.

▲

In the North, earth-maker lichens painting rock,
wet or dry, work their slow transforming art
where the Witch Tree rises from Superior.

Even this huge water body shrinks in drought,
spreads new rocky platforms, makes new shore. Earth
rules dry times. Mosses turn grey tinder,

pine duff crunches on the path. In night skies
across the trees, lightning threatens fire, not rain.
Strange dry season. Anchored to a reef and firm

volcanic ridge, the Susie Islands still ride
the bay, clear water beats in hollowed cliffs along
Hat Point, loons call on the breeze. Look up

where old ice-and-wind carved, twisted root and trunk,
Ma-ni-do Cedar, Spirit Tree, defies a drought
and greens against odds in the sun again this spring.

Wind

SPIRIT TREE TORSO III

THE SPIRIT

Before the Anishinabeg turn east to the great island of plenty, the canoes stop in a group near the end of the point. *No-ko-mis*, Grandmother cedar, leans over them where they sit in their frail birch bark craft. They look up at her, *Ma-ni-do Gee-zhi-gance*, Spirit Little Cedar Tree.

Twenty-two miles of open water, to *Minong* on the horizon, stretch behind the people as they face the rocky point to greet *Ma-ni-do* Cedar and ask for help. Underwater spirits may erupt with wind and high seas. Sudden storms could lash and swamp the canoes.

The chief elder rises in his canoe and prays to the Great Spirit for safe journey:

> *You made the land, the sky, the water.*
> *You placed us, your children, in the world.*
> *You can see fit to unleash forces against our safe journey.*
> *We pray you to keep the Great Lake calm while your children paddle swiftly to Minong.*

He reminds the Great Spirit why they travel, who they are, how they trust the Great *Ma-ni-do*. At last he offers tobacco, *ah-say-ma*, before Spirit Little Cedar Tree to ask for intercession with the Powerful Ones. The Anishinabeg can feel the power as they sit in the canoes and listen to the eloquent words of their elder.

When he has finished speaking and has scattered tobacco over the water near the Spirit Tree, each canoe follows him and makes a tobacco offering. He begins to sing, and the little flotilla turns toward the east, starts the journey into the sunrise.

▲ ▲ ▲

The Anishinabeg knew the fickle lake conditions that made them respect Lake Superior, and they told stories of spirits they considered responsible for lake weather. The stunted cedar tree on Hat Point stands alone, twisted by lake storms and roughened by winter ice as though powerful underwater creatures have reached up and grasped for it. The Witch Tree survives, a natural spirit place for prayers, song and gifts. Tribal people, who understand that everything contains both good and evil, make offerings at spirit places to show respect and honor for all life, to admit that no one knows how long a human life will last. Today, traditional Anishinabeg still make offerings to show honor for animals and fish they hunt, to acknowledge what sustains their own lives.

▲ ▲ ▲

Lying on the porch a few feet from the cliff, lovers hear voices in the river where it runs the rapids below the log cabin.

"Listen. Do you hear singing?"

"Yes. A spirit place."

Women's voices sing the sacred songs that come mysteriously to us where we drift in our world of half-sleep. At just this moment our ears catch the water sound that never stops until winter seals the river flow. This summer night, for the first time, we hear the music.

Long after I learned to listen for river spirits, Hazel introduced me to the Witch Tree. She took me over the snowy path to the lakeshore where ice coated the rocks and sheathed the tree. No one before her had told me about the Spirit Tree, so she could watch my face closely and judge my reaction to this aged stranger I was meeting.

How fragile and small, I think, and yet how strong this No-ko-mis, Grandmother. Bent over, the tree turns toward us where we offer tobacco. Hazel knows each twist of the torso, each twig in the dark topknot of boughs, each fiber that shapes the whole. I look at this miracle of survival posed in its dramatic setting and see brilliant orange lichen on the rocks under ice, clear ice plates shifting on the lake below the tree, the living spirit of the place.

GATHERERS

At night the gatherers plot morning
searches to the berry patch, the bog,
to chanterelles along the trail.
Always the gathering invades their dreams:
fruits tremble on their fingertips,
fungus touched turns into leaves.
Their muscles leap like
startled grouse from alders.
They mutter in their sleep.
Rhythms of the swollen moon and
starry marches map their ways.

Among mountains in pure air,
we speak of freedom, you and I,
our hair bound up in kerchiefs
and the sun hot on our backs.
In the ripeness of wild plenty
we push through thickets
to the center, the largest fruit,
and feel, breathing across the trees,
those other women, gatherers,
our sisters in the ancient rites.

LANGUAGE

What carries culture is the sound
old women breathe in winter time—
stories in grandmother tongue
that rustle from behind the doors,
settle into corners where
firelight can color them.

The way the grandmothers describe
is how the breath of tribes reflects
light from everything that is—
morning mist over the lake,
ropes of chimney smoke that hang
cabins from an evening sky.

Shapes of sound from palate, teeth,
sussuration and the sharp
staccato, the rise and fall
grandmothers use to decorate
the story telling, pattern the mind
the way templates from newspaper

or birchbark—stars, the new moon, leaves,
blossoms—pattern their basketry.
Tribal people recognize
how stories come from the elders
shape intact, but each retelling
unique, alive. The grandmothers

say when someone goes into
the woods and later tells of it,
Anishinabe words describe
each little leaf and twig. The telling
carries back the place, they say.
The words will always keep the place.

SIGNS

Again this fall, like old men's hands
the flat green palms of cedar showed
brownish spots, and deep inside
the maples, chemistry began
withdrawing green. We do not speak
of ordinary signs. We speak
of omens in the sun and moon.

Did you watch the dawn's blue smoke
take the rising golden fire
and smudge it to a bloody eye?
The globe burned low against the islands,
hung until we saw it slowly,
slowly floating to a height
where it could wear its fiery mask.

And listen. What about the moon!
I heard the sheriff's deputy,
old Prowler, tell about the night
he had his breath snatched from his chest.
The dark red moon filled all the sky
from edge to edge and squeezed him flat
behind his steering wheel. He's back
to breathing now, but he's just lucky
that moon lifted when it did.

The elders told us when the fire
readies to vomit from the hills
and deep earth-faults to shift,

birds and small wild creatures leave,
there is a hush, strange fumes escape,
the wells are flooded up.

Who knows which signals telegraph the news?

      Evil is to come
Death
                      Trees laid flat
      Lakes filled in
                      Rivers made of mud and ash
A foul taste in the mouth
                      The fall of kings

CENTER OF THE SPIRIT TREE: VORTEX

DREAMS

I

The fisherman tells of dreams:

Along the deep edge
where the cliffs fall
bald eagles perch.
Far-seeing, great-winged
spirit birds watch me
lift nets, discard fish
held captive for days
when wind whipped the lake
and kept the boats on shore.

I see an eagle stoop
like a flung stone
toward the spoiled catch.
After that day I give
from morning nets a few
fish to feed the curved
talons, the great beak.
I toss onto the water
some part of the catch.

Did you offer yet?
Old Walter asks. He means
tobacco. Didn't think
of it, I say. All day
I ponder how to make

the gift. That night, dreaming,
I plunge my thumb and finger
straight into tobacco.
Then I know how
on dawn's shrouded water
I will sacrifice
ah-say-ma to eagle,
familiar of the air.

II

In waking from dreams, mystery,
in mystery, another world:
I gather something living, leaf
ah-say-ma, to make the gift,

something solid in the hand
that turns, like spirit, like dream,
to smoke and air. The night after
I offer to the eagle I hear,

just as sleep covers me, a sound.
I'm all alone at home, the night
is still, but there's a noise. I check
who wanders in my door—friend for

late talk, neighbor in need? No one.
I go out to the sitting room—
spirit sign, tobacco smoke
lies spread in layers on the air.

III

As the soul's breath is life to putty flesh
and even when we sleep animates
our faces with the look of dreams, so
this world—rock, plants, people, beasts—holds
together with clear breath and air. The face
of every thing alive turns up toward
windy skies, the stars beyond. Should some
great hand crush spirit out, the fragile world
disintegrates and all life is no more.
We know the power: when we surface from
the amniotic wave we scream, we fight
to breathe against the pressure of embrace.
It's wise to tell again our story, make
offering of something living, send
an aromatic smoke into the air.

AT THE FOOT OF THE SPIRIT TREE

GHOSTS

Some fears the old man cherishes.
Just mention owls. He'll tell about
what happened in the sugarbush:

As always, April. Grandma's camp.
Good days, taps dripping in birch bowls,
sap tea, the row of iron kettles
boiling the sugar smell
into our sticky hair. One night
we heard a ghost owl call. Scared,
I'll tell you! We all felt our
skin crawl. No one spoke or stirred
though fire dancers north flared up
light for us. Gathering sap
next morning, we kids found an owl,
long dead, feathers and hollow bones
light as breathing in the hand.

Who was this one? Nobody asked.
Or talked of what it sang at night.
I'm scared to see my own slant eyes,
my hooked beak nose all set about
with feathers in the looking glass,
the painted picture of my ghost.

O W L

This is fear—a face like mine,
black pupil holes in big night-eyes
open to moon shadows, ears
hidden, one turned up, one down
to catch faint murmurings,
a rustle sifting in the grass,
passage of the lightest mice.

This is fear—another's voice
calling like a tinging bell,
a steady drip into the dark,
or deep low-breathing far-off hoots,
then stillness. Suddenly the blunt
feather-body launches out
round head, short wing, pale flash,
from night tree into night.

CHANGE

On the border, the far edge,
we are late, learning
slowly, together, how to live.
We eat wild fruit, rose hips,
forest fungus after rain.
Under pine and rising planets
we lie in each other's arms,
river pulse in our ears. I feel
the shadow of a leaf that falls.
So little time is left to shed
teachings from an alien world,
but I expect to moult and find
myself how like the birds.

Water

WAUS-WAU-GONING BAY

THE PEOPLE

The fisherman remembers the story of his birth:

"Dark spring of the Great Depression, 1930.

"When my mother's pains begin, my dad goes over the Hat Point trail for the midwife, Mrs. Alex Bushman—they called her *Shoo-ni-yonce*.

"The baby takes his time, enters life with the cord wrapped three times around his neck. I am that small strong one. *Shoo-ni-yonce* names me. I am Chief of the Day, *O-ge-ma Gee-zhik*.

"I will dream into the spirit world, travel out of the body, and all my life I will wear the triple mark around my throat."

▲ ▲ ▲

Early French Canadian explorers reported the natural harbor at Grand Portage. Their doing so changed life for Anishinabeg who lived there.

Fur trade companies, recognizing a strategic location, established corporate headquarters on Grand Portage Bay in the 18th century. To supply the fort and the extended network of traders in forests beyond Lake Superior, the companies transported trade goods on the Great Lakes from Montreal to Grand Portage. Voyageurs canoed furs from the back country down to the Fort Charlotte depot on the Pigeon River. The men who brought the trade goods from the east carried them over the Grand Portage Trail to Fort Charlotte and brought the furs down to the lake, where they baled them for the return over the water highway to Montreal. Company boards of directors met in a festive July Rendezvous at the headquarters on Grand Portage Bay and planned the next year's business ventures while the exchange of trade goods and furs took place.

Journals of fur traders in that era mention that the big canoes stopped at Hat Point after the long, dangerous voyage from Montreal. The travelers spruced up their appearance for a triumphal entry around the point into the bay, and they wrote that they made offerings. Indians and French Canadian voyageurs, the essential workers of the fur trade, cooperated closely as trapping and trading associates, and voyageurs married women from the Anishinabe community. No doubt the French Canadians knew the Indians made traditional offerings at

Hat Point to assure safe journey on the treacherous lake. Although the traders' journals do not mention the Spirit Cedar itself, the stop at Hat Point may well have included their thanksgiving offerings at the tree.

During the fur trade era the Anishinabe community at Grand Portage built birch bark canoes for the voyageurs. When the fur traffic through Grand Portage ended and a commercial fishing industry succeeded it in the early decades of the 19th century, local Anishinabeg were hired to harvest the rich fishing waters around Isle Royale for corporate commercial interests. Ruthless exploitation depleted the area's natural resources, the outside business ventures closed down, and the Anishinabeg were left on small reservations—Grand Portage, Minnesota and Fort William, Ontario—to subsist as best they could on government hand-outs. For almost a century the Anishinabeg lived a spare existence.

Powerful forces fostered the exploitation of what had once seemed inexhaustible fish, game, minerals and furs. In 19th century treaty arrangements, entered into unwillingly by the people, the Anishinabeg lost *Minong* and their traditional "wealth," the bountiful gifts of the Great Spirit.

But throughout this time of great change, the Anishinabe culture survived, the story of the *Ma-ni-do* Cedar remained with the people, and the grandmothers continued to tell the children not to play games at the spirit place on Hat Point.

▲ ▲ ▲

There is a funeral, the non-Indian husband of a Band member, and afterward I visit with John.

"Times like that, funerals, weddings, we pay no attention to who's Indian, who isn't," he remarks.

"I don't forget I'm not an Indian," I say, "but I don't feel prejudice from the community."

"Oh," John says, "You're our resident outsider."

I am delighted. We both laugh.

*The pleasure of living here, now nearly two decades, comes in my discovering over and over
again something new and strange—a way of seeing the world, an attitude, a code far
different from my non-Indian heritage. I relish the surprise of having to think outside
my usual self, and I love the stories and laughter, the generosity of my Anishinabe
friends. Living on the Grand Portage Reservation, next to the Pigeon River, near Lake
Superior, is swimming, learning to float, minding the current and the drop-off.
I step into this community as into a deep body of water that bears me up if I will let it.*

NET

A line of floats. A line of lead. Between,
a wall of net. His father dyed it blue.
He sometimes tints it rose or other shade

he has at hand. There's no traditional,
sure-fire dye. Just darken a new net.
Hang any colored fishing wall but white.

Pay it out from anchored float to float—
he keeps his father's places in the bay.
Hang the wall in water where the depth

is set for schools of feeding fish. Mornings,
boats put out from shore to check the catch.
Run nets over the bow and pick, like burrs

from knitted scarves, the gill-hung herring there.
This is a venerable wall, the net—
before the thought of wheels, men knotted mesh.

Such subtle traps. Pygmies on the hunt
in leafy-deep Ituri forest still
set out a line of net for antelope

the way the spider hangs her web for flies
in old economy, a woven wall
set with guile where prey ensnares itself.

The same unheeded chances net us all.
He remembers the time he glanced
from balky motor parts to see Hat Point

go gliding by. So fast a sudden wind
takes up a boat. His brother saw and towed
him in, or else the northwest blow that froze

his motor would have carried him far out.
Too far. Stories the father told call up
the sudden autumn wind, the valiant bend

to oars, the odds against the fisherman
when suddenly wind drops, as lief as not
to let him go. There's an endless shift

and combination to a lake this big—
fog, the fickle wind, under-water
clefts and shallows inter-netted with

the currents, hidden patterns off Hat Point
that swamp a boat in waves. The lake, he says,
will take its share of men who take the fish.

MOUNT ROSE

ELDERS

When your parents grow old
your mother's stories tangle
tongue and teeth in shrunken gums.
Your father hears only
fading whispers of his virtue.
Bloodwhistles through his brain
sing the deafness song.
Like delicate whorled shells,
their subtle colors
fade and grey in the
harsh winter dusk.

Carefully by lamplight
you handle them,
old treaties crumbing yellow edges
at your table.
Deer for their lodge,
driven down freeways, pursued
through aisles and check-out lines,
you bring them.

Change rises and sets,
moves through moons, until you see
your mother staring from the mirror
and you feel her breasts,
her thickened waist,
her thighs under your hands,
and you know at last you
bear and nurture them,
the old ones.

RIDING THE ROAD

Where ravens gather by the road, an eagle
feasts on offal, rises on huge wings
as wheels slow down and approach, rises
to trees leafed with glossy ravens that whet
their bills against the branches—so it seems

to city cyclists dumbfounded near guts
moose hunters left for birds. True bald heads,
turkey vultures, eye these freshly shorn young
athletes sweating up the long incline to stare
the Susie Islands into memory. Stripped

to bikers' second-skins, they concentrate
to circle Lake Superior, to make
their story from the parts—the chilly winds,
rains, hot suns. A retrospective whole
needs the journey's ending to begin.

So too, a man's life lived in these hills
takes form with stories at the funeral lunch.
—Riding out of river valley boyhood,
riding past ravens, eagles, cruising through
years of hunting on beer in beat-up cars

over this same road where vultures wait
the swing of seasons, taking at last the small
important tasks, he was the one who built
the family fires when skies first cleared for frost;
he told the winter tales, joked with friends,

tapped the maples, boiled their sweet lifeblood;
hot August days, he cut firewood
and picked wild raspberries into a cup, one
by one, with his grandchild. The funeral
closed his circle. Now the stories grow.

SURVIVAL

So. Now is time to teach forgotten skills,
Anishinabe ways. Some who hunt
track only from the front seat of the car,
leave moosemeat rotting in the roadside ditch
enough to feed a family a week,
good food, head, ribs for ravens to clean up.
Every month now wise men visit here
who come to us from Canada, the far
cold villages where northern winds have kept
the old skills fresh. Around our fires they tell
the story of what's coming, how the pale
invaders will set off a blast to shake
our mother Earth and blister her. They knew
before the dusty message on the wind
when old St. Helens lava pit would blow,
and they see evil streams to come. Much worse.
Survival is what children need to learn,
how to hole up safe and make it through
poison-wars, the plans of crazy men.
Tribal people can survive who know
what Fox and Raven know, Bear, Caribou.
Those are the skills that count, not chemistry
or fool computer schemes. We need old ways.

GIRL OF THE LAKEHEAD

A dented pail in each hand, Clark's daughter
pauses in the littered dooryard.
Behind her the Canadian bush
lies, a strand of hair across
the snowy fields.

Sturdy in a man's torn parka,
she lifts her head, sniffs the air,
a shaggy pony of a girl
glad for the chance to talk.
She drops opinions like potatoes in a furrow,

flashes a smile of blackened teeth.
Schools, Prime Minister, the Press
break on her cheerful contempt.
It's as though the cities of the nation
flooded in, and when the tide drew back

leaving a line of tin and plastic shells,
she stood where she was planted,
battered some with the detritus, but unmoved.
There's a yelp for water. She shrugs
and takes the worn footpath down to the spring.

BORDER STORY

Who is this tall man in a blue felt hat?
With his attentive entourage, he comes
from fifty years ago, a college kid
who pumped gas on a summer job, then left
the border town until today with no
regret. It was a lonely time, he says,
no other young folks here, just Indians—
the Boss never hired them, of course.
Sold them quarts of beer outside the law.
Old story—let them drink behind his shed,
souse them up, then call them drunken bums.
Useless to try and get an honest day's
work from anyone but whites—a boy
like me still wet behind the ears could moon
away a summer by the pumps, but not
an Indian—that was the Boss's creed.

Under the jaunty blue hatbrim his eyes
are young. Eagerly he searches signs
of gas pumps, cabin where he bunked, the rope
he swung down every night to bathe under
the Pigeon River cliffs. Oh yes, it looks
the same, he says, not minding what is gone—
cafe, bridge, Standard Oil sign,
Greyhound bus garage, the Customs house—
seeing, instead, the truth of tales he's told:
a lonely summertime before the War
when he was nineteen on the edge of life.
Today with ease he finds the border days

he lived here long ago, as though each were
a piece of shale he picks up and skims
flat on the water, thin young back naked
to the red sun setting in the gorge,
his fingers turning blue in rain run-off,
crayfish nipping at his toes, a whistled
otter-call, night coming on, years.

HARD FROST

In the garden, vines are sprawling wet,
freighted with green tomatoes, summer squash
too tough to eat. Overnight they meet
the end of fruiting, end of flowering.
The pall settles as it always does
too soon in this short-season place.
Fruit unripened by retreating sun
darkens in the morning cold. What slugs
don't eat will drop and melt into the earth.

Harry has to shoot his crippled dog,
frail as a great-grandmother, joints seized,
prey to all the aches of age, her bark
perfunctory, her patience a reproach.
Hard frost is coming. He refuses friends
wanting to spare him, willing to kill old Girl
out at the dump. She needs her burial,
he says, and runs his hand over the pain.
The earth will do the rest and take her in.

▲

Winter shows its talons one last time,
threatens the end of June. Harry reports
the meadowland around his place is white
with frost. A strange spring—early warmth and bloom,
then cold come late, he says. As if on cue
the balsam poplars snow the next three days.
Cotton drifts along the path, settles,

gives snowy light under the moon. It hangs
festooned from cobwebs, catches on the rough

board windowsills, gathers in open sheds
where mice and voles line their nests. The poplars
imitate at solstice, under the long
summer sun, the axis tilt ahead,
the spume of flakes in early winter dusk.
Harry has started his deathward Journey twice
and twice returned more fragile, more aware,
but after he marks this cotton storm, this late
sharp frost, he slips all seasons at last.

ICE BREAK, SPIRIT TREE

PASSAGE

I

Carved full-bodied, the woman
stands on the window sill above us,
her wooden breasts curved heavy
like the waning moon,
beaded ears and necklace, flat
broad cheek, hand against her thigh.
Through spruce branches
moon flows in its milky wash
where we lie shaped
into each other's bones,
our old flesh soft.

She bears beauty scars in threes,
light-rays from her navel,
from corners of her purse of lips,
and down the lovely curve
of breasts to where the tips are rubbed.
House totem far from home,
her dark wood alien,
she waits, impassive
patron of our rites.

What has happened on the way,
the long years to this night?
I see you paled by moonlight,
shadow hair scarred on your body.
I cannot believe in our initiation—

we were always here, touching
thighs and shoulders,
sleepy after love, ageless
as household gods.

II

You are old and come to this:
that you are patient while the plot
reveals its convolutions to the end.
Here is the maze you entered,
your linen thread like a trail
laid down by snails at night
on sandy garden paths. No one
can break its long-ago unrolled
reminder that the end is to go
back where you began, where you tied
the careful knot you learned in Scouts,
slipped it like a ring of promise
on your thumb, and started out.
Each alone we come to this, you know.

Do you hear me singing? Calling
your name through the labyrinth?
Is there perfume in the air?
Yes, I go this way alone before you,
I, too, rewinding loops of yarn
over my half-opened palm,
pushing through the privet alleys

toward an entry gate I may remember.
Abandonment in the air like mist
draws its wash on every cusp of leaf.
What we found, each, at the center,
darkness in its green hold,
follows, did you notice,
follows us out.

III

Shall we sit here on this Persian
rug of moss and lichen? The river
like a knife cuts Precambrian rock
for us alone, and from its gorge
ages rise like mists that shawl

the rounded shoulders of these hills.
Across the maple ridge morning
leafed bare branches pink,
and in the evening the Royal Island east
will blush and glow, its ridges copper

in the setting sun, its rock cliffs
burning on the water. Here in what's
left of a new world, we keep watch—
daily fading of the other's face,
grey misting in our hair. We feel

clods of earth fill in around us.

What our kind calls time
and dimly comprehends with clocks
moves in us like blood,
the marvel and the limit of our lives.

Fire

SPIRIT TREE TORSO I

THE ART

It's 1922. A young blond fellow stares eagerly at the rugged lake shore as the steamship America docks at Pete's Island. "This is the place!"

He disembarks with his painter's gear and the next morning negotiates for a boat to row across to the mainland. There he rents a log cabin from Leonard Hendrickson, a Swedish immigrant who was fishing commercially with his brother Sven Herman in Waus-wau-goning Bay, off Hat Point and the Susie Islands.

Dewey Albinson, the city artist, is looking for a place to paint undisturbed. He's excited by the dramatic scenery of Grand Portage, the large bay rimmed with hills, the rough rock coast, the "picturesque shacks" of the Indian residents. Leonard alerts him to John Clemont, *May-au-say*, an Indian elder, who talks about an old tree in a nearby cove. When he investigates the site by boat, all Albinson can say is "Glory be!" His exclamation is an unconscious echo of prayers and offerings the cedar tree inspired for centuries before him. People tell him evil lurks near the tree, a dark bird of ill omen in its branches. He paints the dramatic little cedar, listens to stories of its spiritual significance and supplies his own understanding of good and evil.

▲ ▲ ▲

Twenty years later, the Minneapolis *Sunday Tribune* printed a reproduction of an Albinson painting called "The Witch Tree." The title entered into common usage, and among the Anishinabeg of Grand Portage today the Spirit Cedar is referred to as the Witch Tree. There is fear still associated with it, but the tree itself is not thought of as evil. Visitors to the Witch Tree respond instinctively with awe, as Albinson did, as tribal people have always done. Its setting at the edge of the huge lake—the great rocks, the orange and green lichen, the wide expanse of water, islands floating off shore—attracts tourists, artists, and naturalists.

Albinson's interest in preserving Lake Superior's north shore history and natural beauty prompted his work during the 1930's with the Minnesota Historical Society and other organizations. He was disgruntled when modern housing began to replace the Reservation's "picturesque shacks," and the new log school built in 1939 on the bluff above the bay dismayed him. When Highway 61 was rerouted near the lake to cut through Moose Pass at Mount

Josephine, he worked in vain to prevent the change. He lived to bemoan the large numbers of tourists he himself had attracted to the natural phenomenon he called the Witch Tree. Although he feared damage to the fragile tree, artists from around the world have followed him in a tradition of respect and inspiration at the Grand Portage *Ma-ni-do Gee-zhi-gance*.

▲ ▲ ▲

The last day of the season, we go on board the M/V Wenonah at 6:30, a rainy evening in early September. This is a special voyage, a gift to Grand Portagers, and many of our Indian friends are passengers on the cruise through the Susie Islands. Tourists have been making this excursion in summer sunsets to enjoy scenic, historic Waus-wau-goning Bay. Beautiful days fall either side of our trip, but we are fated to have a low sky, intermittent rain, the air chilly enough to keep my hands deep in my parka pockets and the hood pulled up.

I stand next to Herman in the bow. He fishes these waters daily, year after year, yet he rides the Wenonah tonight for a holiday. We round Hat Point and he shows me the cliff where eagles perch, the cabin where he and Penny began their married life.

The captain slows the ship and moves in closer to shore. "The Witch Tree," he announces on his loudspeaker. Suddenly there is silence on board. Everyone turns toward the grey presence that stands forth from the forest and casts its reflection on the water. I am surprised and moved by how powerful the tree looks from the lake. No one speaks until the engine resumes speed and we head into the islands along the inner passage.

PARTRIDGE FALLS

I truly believe art can save the world.
      Hazel Belvo, painter

Just before the water gathers force
and pulls its weight together for the edge,
the rock dam and the fall, a ledge shows
ripples left where water ran on sand
millennia ago. Volcanic rock
that covered here breaks along the fault,
so as we squat beside the Pigeon River
and current pushes past us toward the fall
where rare ferns flourish briefly in the mist,
other power rises in the spray
heavy with a future from long ago.
We smell, under the pinch of balsam green
and fresh brown river scent, the water
of another eon laying out life rich
in possibilities, the magma flow,
steam rising and the glimpse ahead—us
gathered by the river fingering
the ripple-carving, old under our hands.
What chance we'll leave a mark like this in sand
that runs like river through our glass? Water
rippling casts a stony shadow here
fixed by heat and weight. Through catastrophic
shifts and change—almost casual
survival of this ledge—a rhythmic shape
that should be lost, as any form in sand,
stays in beauty for us, and in art.

NAME

Soon I have a 28"x36" painting. I entitle it "The Witch Tree."
And the tree has been known by this name ever since.
      Dewey Albinson, painter—manuscript memoir

A youth rebels against parental rule,
and yet his course is set with charts from home.
The myths he learned in childhood split the world,
an apple in Eve's hand, bad and good
forever setting Adam's teeth on edge.
It's simple—evil must be overcome,

and that is how he understands the tree,
a giant bird of omen in its hair.
Springtime in salt Atlantic spray, he's read,
fisherfolk still weave hawthorne boughs,
ash blossom for the face, and make a witch,
a European way to greet the waves.

All night the green witch grows monstrous, strong,
and when the women weavers have fulfilled
the ritual, men heave the gift at dawn
off the cliff into the sea. Stone-weighted,
the green witch sinks deep where storms and winds
receive the offering—awareness, fear.

The artist listens to Ojibway tales—
tobacco for *Ma-ni-do Gee-zhi-gance*,
gifts offered at the Spirit Tree to calm
the great lake when the birch canoes set out.

All ships are frail, he thinks, all seas wild.
From a rowboat on the bay, he draws the tree,

a throne of rock, sees a woman-shape
twisted toward the water, woven branches,
trunk and root powerful against
rough wind, waves, freezing spray. Nearby,
the fisherman's cabin, where he sleeps, leans
toward gales from northeast, winter, ice.

All summer he listens. He hears no
bravado. Honor for nature he shares
and tries to catch in paint and pencil: trees,
cabins, people, wild north shore. But when
he paints the *Ma-ni-do*, he hears his own
echo name his painting *The Witch Tree*.

THE ROOT OF THE SPIRIT TREE

TURNING

Woodturners release the spirit of the tree.
      Mary Thouin, wood artist

Out of years ringing, the round
and the laying of color. Out of roots
and the season, growing, sap running.
Out of the mischief of weather, dead branches,
the knotting of fibres, the burl. Under
bark cover, imagine the healing.
Out of the fire and wasting, green
pushing through rocks, the encircling.
Out of charred root through the crevices, new
holding the old and the shaping.
Out of the deep secret life, spirit speaking.

LENS

I've never wanted to learn about my roots before.
       Rick Novitsky, photographer—hearing his surname is common in Moscow

The grandfather was born in the Ukraine.
A bad place in a bad time. A kid
was happy to shake its dusty fields

from emigrating boots. He told Rick's dad,
Forget it, Son. No, I never want
to see again where I was a boy.

No tug of memory to tell a tale,
no snapshots to blur in idle tears,
he died before the grandson knew to ask.

▲

Shutter open to the Spirit Tree
winter and summer, good weather and foul,
Rick sees, with a camera's eye, fire

dancing across the north, a painted moon
pale on the blue world, mist that draws
red from the water at dawn. Waiting

for lightning whiplashes to strike the sky,
he feels the root's clutch in the granite,
the trunk's twist, the fragility of strength.

▲

Where it comes from? How grows this old tree?
The Moscow visitor opens wide
his arms, embraces the horizon. Rick

takes a guess: shoots creeping toward sunlight,
the green force widening cracks in the rock,
lasting through storm lash, wind, even fire—

new shoots crowning, clinging to the dead,
over and over re-braiding the trunk,
staying through seasons—green beyond green.

The camera tracks from the head's tangled
branches, down the torso in its frozen
sheath, to the foot and founding rock

bright with orange lichen, ice and sun.
Rick sees the old world focusing the new,
the lens from Russia pointing toward the roots.

HORIZON

I'm trying to see beyond the edge of the world, beyond the unknown.
        George Morrison, painter

Long line where the world folds,
float-line of the imagination,
mark dividing fear from pluck,
rim of life and death,
time's edge rising
slowly on the unknown,
source of sun and moon over
great water, cold
mystery, furnace of fire,

horizon, his obsession, lies across each
canvas, notebook sketch, collage.
A boy could sit for hours
on the stony beach counting stars,
watching a shadow of eclipse
slowly eat the silver globe until
the lighted lake-path straight
toward horizon from the shore
grows dim and disappears.

Fog smoking over water draws
horizon in, the edge a mere
arm's reach beyond ghost rocks;
tethered islands slip their anchor,
shrouded water stretching
toward the boy's familiar shoal

becomes mysteriously
unknown,
a drifting shadow.

Sun at the enigmatic line,
fire palette, burns the red
rock cliff and osier branch.
Wind brushes water. Sky color
shifts—rock and lake respond.
Beyond the unknown,
endless, rises
recreated change, the living
substance of his art.

From the deep remembering, he lets
each way he works the paint
create a landscape: shore, sky, lake,
color, horizontal space,
the long line in the hand.

N O - K O - M I S

But, sitting here, I know that this is
Grandma, old and gnarled.
            Barton Sutter, poet—"Witch Tree"

I

In the North Shore Hospital
the old ones cannot navigate
the long night voyage without machines
to tow them through the troughs of pain.

No-ko-mis, faithful widow,
ninety-three, crochets acrylic
shawls and waits. Carefully
she lies back on the bed, murmurs,

admonishes herself, whispers
to the black-braided girl she was,
waiting dockside on Pete's Island,
watching the ship America's

hold unloaded, learning omens.
Her steady whispered hiss unravels
old webs of lists, lies, fears, against
the shuttle pacemaker threading

fidelity through fitful sleeps,
through birthwails blowing down the hall,
wind at cedar boughs, storm cries
in rigging of the ship she waits.

II

Poets and artists see a woman's trunk,
hip jutting against storms, arms raised, root-feet
gripping the rock crevices, a girl
grown old in an unlikely place. The way
a woman comes back from the birthing bed,
the cedar yields, retreats, then returns

misshapen, somehow stronger, powerful,
willing each survival. Hazel paints
a portrait of her standing self, her arms
uplifting her son's daughter overhead.
She paints the woman's triumph as a tree,
the power bearing fruit beyond her time.

III

Spirit Cedar, Witch Tree on Hat Point,
wind dancer, wild with hair of thunderbirds,
bowsprit breasting seas, grain weathered
all shades of grey, girl young long ago,
who stood the storms of waiting for her love,
old woman, grandmother, *No-ko-mis*,
wise wealth of years, strong bones, survivor, source.

SPIRIT TREE TORSO IV: NO-KO-MI S

AFTERWORD

In 1987 members of the Grand Portage community joined in a group called Friends of the Witch Tree under the leadership of Rick Novitsky and Bill Corcoran. Hazel Belvo and Joanne Hart were part of the organizing group. Within two and a half years, fund raising efforts allowed Friends of the Witch Tree to purchase the land where the old cedar tree still stands looking much as it did in photographs taken more than half a century ago. In 1990, the tree and its site were turned over to the Grand Portage Chippewa Band for permanent preservation as a spirit place.

Visitors to the tree drive out past the log school house almost to the end of Hat Point where there is a parking lot. Signs direct them to the Witch Tree path, a short walk through woods to an observation post on the rock coast overlooking Waus-wau-goning Bay. With publicity developed by the fund drive, there has been an increase in the number of visitors to the tree. Concerned about preservation, the Grand Portage Tribal Government has built a dramatic new approach to the tree and erected signs to explain its spiritual significance and draw attention to the respect this unusual tree demands. The Anishinabe name, *Ma-ni-do Gee-zhi-gance*, expresses the mystery and power of the tree. The common name, Witch Tree, has been adopted for familiar use by local residents and visitors alike.

From all over the United States and from England, Holland, Mexico, Canada and the Soviet Union, donors responded to the appeal for funds to purchase the Witch Tree site and its access. Many expressed a wish to preserve natural beauty and wrote of their respect for the old ways of tribal peoples, who understand the connections between humans and the world around them. The people of Grand Portage still place the traditional gifts of tobacco, ribbon and vermilion to honor the spirit power of *Ma-ni-do Gee-zhi-gance*.

Joanne Hart, born in Weehawken, New Jersey, says she "turned Minnesotan" in 1949 when she graduated from the College of St. Catherine and began living in St Paul. She was a Fellow in 1985 at the Atlantic Center for the Arts where William Stafford was her mentor. Since 1974 her home has been a remote part of the Grand Portage Indian Reservation by the Pigeon River, the border between northeastern Minnesota and Ontario, Canada. There she is "pretty quiet" during the academic year when her husband teaches 400 miles from home. Now that her eight children are adults, she takes pleasure in setting her own schedule. Her poems and essays appear in many magazines and journals, and she has three chapbooks of poetry: *In These Hills* (1983) and *I Walk on the River at Dawn* (1986), both from Women's Times Publishing, and *The Village Schoolmaster* (1985) from The Bieler Press. She and Hazel Belvo have another collaborative work in progress about *No-ko-mis*, the Grandmother.

Hazel Belvo, born in Southern Ohio in 1934, says her mother and her Dutch grandmother "are the rocks and roots in my life." She was a Mary Ingraham Bunting Institute Scholar at Radcliffe College. Her work has been shown nationwide and internationally, as well as in museums and galleries in New York and Minnesota, and her paintings and drawings are in private collections around the world. There have been many major exhibitions of parts of her "Meditation on the Spirit Tree," most recently in a national exhibition, "Deep Woods," traveling to eight states. An artist-teacher, a WARM mentor and a faculty member of the Grand Marais Art Colony, she is Associate Professor and Chair of the Division of Fine Arts at the Minneapolis College of Art and Design. From her studios at Red Rock on the Grand Portage Indian Reservation and Minneapolis, she conducts workshops in making personal art. Hazel Belvo is the mother of three sons, Joseph and Daniel Belvo and Briand Mesaba Morrison.